first book about animals

of the plains

For a free color catalog describing Gareth Stevens'
list of high-quality books and multimedia programs,
call 1-800-542-2595 (USA) or 1-800-461-9120 (Canada).
Gareth Stevens Publishing's Fax: (414) 225-0377.

Library of Congress Cataloging-in-Publication Data available upon
request from publisher. Fax: (414) 225-0377 for the attention of
the Publishing Records Department.

ISBN 0-8368-2651-5

This North American edition first published in 2000 by
Gareth Stevens Publishing
1555 North RiverCenter Drive, Suite 201
Milwaukee, WI 53212 USA

© QA International, 1999
Additional end matter © 2000 by Gareth Stevens, Inc.

Created and produced as *visit the animals
on the plains* by QA International,
329 rue de la Commune Ouest, 3e étage,
Montréal, Québec, Canada H2Y 2E1.
Tel.: (514) 499-3000 Fax: (514) 499-3010
www.qa-international.com

Printed in the United States of America

1 2 3 4 5 6 7 8 9 04 03 02 01 00

Gareth Stevens Publishing
MILWAUKEE

The zebra is running away...

at a gallop.

The leopard is climbing...

in the trees.

A mother giraffe is keeping an eye on...

her baby giraffe.

The dromedary is walking around...

in the desert.

The rhinoceros is carrying...

his friends, the birds.

The baby elephant is staying...

very close to its mother.

The cheetah is running...

very fast.

Glossary

cheetah — a large, wild, spotted cat from Africa that can run at great speed.

climb — to move upward.

desert — a hot, dry, sandy area that gets little or no rain.

dromedary — a camel with one hump.

friends — people you like and enjoy spending time with.

gallop — to run fast.

zebra — a wild animal from Africa that has black-and-white stripes and the shape of a horse.

Index